THE
Archive Photographs
SERIES
JUNKERS
A Pioneer In Aviation

Born 3 February 1859, Hugo Junkers was interested in engineering at an early age but had reached fifty before becoming involved in aviation. However, the company which bore his name went on to build the first all-metal aeroplane and Junkers proved to be a visionary in many other ways. Indeed, his innovations clearly influenced the development of air transport and have earned him an honoured place in aviation history.

THE
Archive Photographs
SERIES

JUNKERS
A PIONEER IN AVIATION

Compiled by
Brian Walters

CHALFORD

First published 1997
Copyright © Brian Walters, 1997

The Chalford Publishing Company
St Mary's Mill, Chalford,
Stroud, Gloucestershire, GL6 8NX

ISBN 0 7524 0742 2

Typesetting and origination by
The Chalford Publishing Company
Printed in Great Britain by
Redwood Books, Trowbridge

Cover illustration
During the 1930s, the Ju 52 became the workhorse of the Lufthansa fleet and some
are seen here on the apron at Berlin's Tempelhof Airport. The German airline's Ju
52 active fleet numbered nearly eighty examples but although some 230 were
registered in its name, many were flown by other operators.

Contents

Introduction

Today it may seem curious that a man who did not become actively involved in aviation until he was fifty years old, should have become such a visionary and exercised considerable influence in the design and operation of aircraft. However, it must be remembered that once the principle of heavier-than-air flight had been proved, it was inevitable that those with an inventive turn of mind should be attracted to the new science.

And so it was with Professor Hugo Junkers who, during the late 1890s, built up a successful business producing heating equipment, industrial boilers and temperature gauges, for which he employed thousands of workmen at his factory in Dessau, Germany. Other pioneers in aviation were also attracted to aviation in their mature years, so in this respect there was nothing unusual about Junkers. The French engineer Gustave Eiffel for example, is best remembered for his tower in Paris but he also developed an interest in aerodynamics, later designing a wind tunnel to probe new designs.

Certainly Junkers was never happier than when he was carrying out research and by 1892, had already been granted his first patent – for an apparatus which could measure the calorific value of liquid and gas fuels. Indeed, it was because no-one wanted to produce one of his patented heaters that Junkers set up his own manufacturing facility.

In later years, Junkers acknowledged that he had been interested in flight from an early age but could not spare the time to become involved. After all, as a married man with a family (which was to grow to six sons and six daughters), Junkers had to earn a living and it was almost by chance that he became actively involved with aircraft design and construction. A fellow professor at Aachen Technical High School invited his collaboration on an aircraft project in 1909 and the rest, as they say, is history. However, it is still remarkable that at such an early stage in the development of aviation, a man with absolutely no experience in aerodynamics and

To counter misgivings expressed by some concerning the safety of an all-metal cantilever wing, Junkers had forty-two workers stand upon an unsupported J 3 wing built in 1916.

aircraft construction, should have concluded that an all-metal low-wing monoplane with a hollow wing was the optimum formula for a successful aeroplane.

It was during his time as a professor at Aachen that Junkers began to study aerodynamics, the enterprising High School having established a wind tunnel to encourage research. Junkers however, was not content with the school's wind tunnel so he had one built for his own use at nearby Frankenburg, although after he gave up teaching, he built another one at Dessau.

In the period between 1914 and 1919, it is said that Junkers carried out studies on some 400 models, conducting about 4,000 tests to measure the lift and drag performance of different wing designs. One conclusion that Junkers drew was that thick profile wings could be surprisingly efficient, a view shared by Eiffel and others who had conducted similar tests.

Showing remarkable courage and self-confidence, Junkers decided to become the first to build an all-metal monoplane with no external struts or wires supporting the wing. Some of his friends reproached him for deliberately facing ruin by using money earned from making heating equipment on such a frivolous enterprise. Nevertheless, Junkers carried out experiments in the construction of an all-metal wing and the outbreak of war in 1914, suddenly brought the attention of a military commission to his work. Consequently, Junkers received an order to produce a trials aircraft – which became the J 1 of 1915.

It takes a man of vision and determination to pioneer new methods of design and construction, whatever the product may be, and Hugo Junkers certainly had these qualities. However, he was also a man who was unwilling to share control and, like so many of his ilk, really preferred to undertake research and solve problems rather than set about the quantity production of the end result. So while Anthony Fokker produced thousands of combat aircraft during the First World War, Hugo Junkers developed interesting designs but built only a couple of hundred J 4 reconnaissance aircraft for the Luftwaffe.

As well as manufacturing aircraft, Junkers produced some engines at the Dessau works where they became known as 'Jumo' engines, a contraction of 'Junkers Motorenbau.' Indeed, Professor Hugo Junkers (centre) had begun to develop a gas engine as early as 1892 and continued to produce heating equipment when demand for aircraft slowed.

The factory at Dessau continued to function as the prime source of Junkers aircraft, long after the death of its founder on 3 February 1935.

He preferred to be a scientist and entrepreneur, rather than a businessman, although it must be said that after the First World War, he turned his attention to the development of civil air transport with typical determination and single-mindedness.

Nevertheless, although the F 13 and the Ju 52 were to become the classic airliners of their time in the period 1919 to 1932, the development of aircraft at Dessau tended to be unprofitable because comparatively few reached large-scale production. Indeed, of thirty-seven projects embarked upon in this period, only eleven were produced in quantity. As a result, the company was often in financial difficulties and although the world economic recession clearly had an effect on business, Junkers himself was responsible for much of the problem.

Alas, it is the nature of aviation that many aircraft designers and airline owners seem to be oblivious of the need to make money, taking the view that it is far more interesting to solve technical problems or open new routes, than to spend time making sure that the enterprise is profitable. So Junkers is by no means alone in this respect and whatever his failings, his place in aviation history is assured.

However, it would be wrong to conclude that Junkers had absolutely no business sense because if this were so, he would not have overcome the tangle of regulations which, although designed to prevent the construction of military aircraft in Germany after the First World War, also hindered civil aircraft production. Indeed, the F 13 quickly fell victim to this and the Allies were evidently confused as to its status, first of all authorising the use of the 'Junkers metal limousine' but later imposing a ban on its export.

Convinced of the potential for air transport to forge links between nations but responding to slow demand for the F 13, Junkers decided either to form airlines or make a significant contribution to the establishment of new carriers. Thus, in November 1920, Lloyd Ostflug was founded with financial backing from Junkers and within a month an air mail service was inaugurated between Berlin and Konigsberg via three other stops.

A Polish airline supported by Junkers followed and gradually the number of airlines backed by the company increased until by 1925, the Europa-Union was formed by an international alliance of no less than sixteen European airlines. However, further development was inhibited by the formation of Luft Hansa in 1926 at the urging of the German government which was anxious to cut back on subsidies. This brought together Junkers Luftverkehr and German Aero Lloyd.

Undaunted, Junkers went on to find applications for the F 13 in other parts of the world and in 1926, was granted a five-year monopoly to operate air services in Persia, commencing operations with Junkers Luftverkehr Persien the following year. But in 1922 an even more significant event had taken place when Russia's Soviet government signed an agreement with Junkers under which the company undertook to produce all-metal aircraft at Fili, a site near Moscow.

For this, Junkers received funds from the German War Ministry which wanted to encourage commercial ventures abroad, although when the Nazis came to power in 1933, this policy was to be reversed. Nevertheless, during the period in which Junkers ran the Fili plant, a total of 170 all-metal aircraft were built and he had established an aircraft industry for the Soviet Union. Both military and civil Junkers types were supplied to meet Soviet needs, while Dobrolyot – an airline formed in 1923 – ultimately operated 24 F 13s.

In an endeavour to overcome the limitations imposed by the Versailles Treaty, Junkers tried to interest Henry Ford in the licence-production of the G24 but when this failed, he turned to Sweden where Adrian and Carl Florman had established an airline equipped with a pair of F 13s. They were keen to form a closer relationship with Junkers and the upshot was the formation of an aircraft manufacturing factory in Limhamn near Malmo.

Ostensibly a totally Swedish venture formed with the approval of its government, A.B. Flygindustrie was in fact financially, as well as technically supported by Junkers, and its first role was to convert G 23s to the more powerful G 24 configuration, as well as convert the A 20 to a bomber role for Turkey. Indeed, Limhamn effectively but covertly became the military branch of Junkers, developing aircraft for delivery or production at Fili in Russia or in Japan where Mitsubishi was the licence-holder.

Note: The designations given to Junkers-designed aircraft may seem confusing but the following list of prefixes provides some explanation:

J and later Ju – Junkers
F   –   single-engined transport
K   –   light transport or combat
T   –   sports/research/touring
H   –   adapted for military use – produced in Russia
A   –   low-wing, open cockpit civil/military
G   –   multi-engined (three or more) transport
W   –   seaplane
S   –   special
EF   –   experimental

One

From 'Corrugated Iron Duck' to the First Warplanes

While history justifiably accords the Wright Brothers with being the first to produce a practical heavier-than-air machine which could fly under its own power, hundreds of others around the world had worked toward the same goal. On a trial and error basis, inventors and aeronauts had experimented unsuccessfully before the young Americans triumphed but, inspired by their example, they quickly set about extending the frontiers of aviation knowledge.

Although interested in flight, Professor Hugo Junkers was not one of them. Throughout his adult life he had taken a strong interest in engineering, his company manufacturing such products as radiators, gas-powered engines and gas-fired boilers. However, he was also a professor at the Technical High School in Aachen where he taught thermodynamics and indeed, it was there that Junkers became first involved in aviation. A fellow professor at Aachen, Hans Reissner, had carried out experiments in the design and construction of flying machines, producing a bi-plane in 1909 but after this was destroyed in a crash, he collaborated with Junkers on further experiments. Nevertheless Junkers acknowledges that because he had little time to spare, the result of their co-operation was largely due to Reissner's work.

Junkers' contribution took the form of a metal wing constructed from corrugated sheet iron and in Reissner's monoplane design this was located at the rear of the fuselage, with the control surfaces positioned at the front. As a result of using what is known as the canard configuration (which is coming back into favour today), Reissner's aircraft became known as the corrugated iron duck and in 1912 it made several successful flights. The aircraft crashed in the following year but by then Junkers' interest in aviation had been stimulated and he demonstrated his grasp of aerodynamics and foresight by patenting a hollow wing form which, together with corrugated sheeting, was to become a feature of his designs. Although ridiculed for wanting to build an all-metal aircraft which would be heavier than those made from wood and fabric, Junkers was not to be dissuaded and obstinately stuck to the concept. Plumbers and other engineers more used to producing boilers were put to building metal aeroplanes, and the J 1 'tin donkey' produced in 1915, set the pattern for other military aircraft which emerged from the Dessau workshops thereafter.

However, although a number of monoplane designs were produced over the next couple of years, it was the J 4 sesqui-plane which became the first Junkers aircraft to be built in quantity. (A sesqui-plane is a bi-plane in which the lower wing has less than half the area of the upper wing).

Nicknamed the 'tin donkey' the experimental J 1 was the world's first all-metal aircraft and it flew for the first time (to the astonishment of some) on 12 December 1915.

The cantilever wing was unorthodox at a time when struts, wires and other forms of external bracing were commonplace, but the iron-clad J 1 had proved the concept and it was followed in 1916 by the J 2, a single-seat fighter design of which only three were built. The J 2 was also of sheet iron construction, although Junkers would have preferred to use aluminium sheeting, then in short supply.

Derived from the J 2, only one J 3 fighter was built but it never flew. However, more than 200 examples of the J 4 two-seat patrol sesqui-plane (seen here) were built and introduced into service in early 1917. It was unusual in having an armoured fuselage.

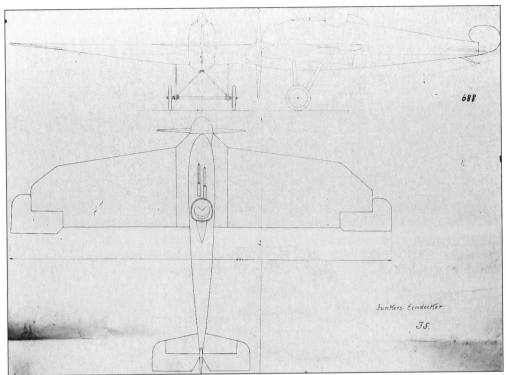

While series production of the J 4 was under way, the company began design work on the J 5 single-seat fighter but problems with engine cooling prevented further development.

Construction of the high-wing J 6 was incomplete when the Armistice ended the First World War in November 1918 but the J 7 fighter seen here, with the now familiar corrugated duralumin skin preferred by Junkers, crashed at the hands of Anthony Fokker before it could complete trials in a fighter competition. Fokker's entry won!

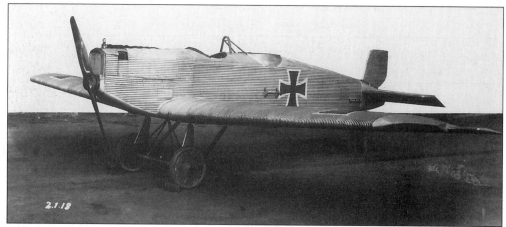

The two-seat J 8 was developed from the J 9 as a close-support aircraft and featured a lengthened fuselage as well as an increased wing span. However only one example of this remodelled J 9 was built and flown in 1918.

Developed from the J 7, the J 9 single-seat fighter incorporated a number of improvements which resulted in a considerably enhanced performance; in particular it had a higher top speed and was more manoeuvrable. Although the J 9 flew for the first time only in March 1918, more than forty saw service before the war ended and some later served with volunteer units fighting Bolshevik forces in Finland, Estonia and Lithuania.

The J 10 was a further development of the J 8 and although more than forty had been built for ground attack roles by the end of the First World War, only a few saw active service. After the war some were converted to carry a single passenger in place of the observer.

Only three examples of the J 11 naval patrol seaplane were built but after its first flight in the summer of 1918, it was too late for production orders to be placed following the signing of the Armistice. However, when an Imperial Navy pilot conducted trials in October 1918, he described the performance of the J 11 as 'outstanding, the rate of climb for a seaplane being unsurpassed.' The example seen here is fitted with a wheeled undercarriage.

The first multi-seat all-metal airliner, the F 13 was designed in 1919 by Otto Reuter and it went on to become a widely-used airliner which also established a number of world records.

Two
The First All-Metal Airliner

It is hard to believe that a four-seat aircraft could be described now as an 'airliner,' yet the Junkers F 13 became the means by which many air carriers were launched in the 1920s and few historians today would dispute the claim that it was the prototype commercial aeroplane.

When the Armistice was declared in November 1918, Professor Junkers announced that future efforts were to be concentrated on civil projects and decided that a totally new aircraft should be produced. Nevertheless, the F 13 would benefit from the experience which the company had gained from the production of all-metal designs but it would also have to compete with bargains from among the many converted military aircraft then flooding the market. So the F 13 was expected to offer something special that would distinguish it from the new designs then emerging from the drawing boards of other companies, as they also switched from military aircraft production.

At a time when fabric-covered, wooden-framed construction was a widely used method and many aircraft companies had not progressed beyond bi-plane designs, the F 13 employed structural and aerodynamic techniques that were far ahead of their time. The result was an aircraft which was robust, adaptable and reliable – qualities which attracted orders from many parts of the world, although when sales were slow initially, Junkers was not averse to boosting production by helping in the formation of new airlines. Indeed, the company became one of the first to employ this method of getting its products into the hands of operators and to accelerate the process, in 1921 it formed its own airline; Junkers Lufverkehr acquiring no less than sixty F 13s within two years. By means of investments, the provision of free loans or even outright gifts of aircraft, Junkers helped in the formation of sixteen European carriers, while the establishment of a world height record by the F 13 prototype in 1919 stimulated widespread interest in the new aircraft.

However, the F 13 became the subject of disputes with the Inter-Allied Control Commission which had been established to ensure that the provisions of the Versailles Treaty were observed by Germany. Signed after the First World War, the Treaty imposed limitations intended to prevent the production of military equipment in Germany, a long list of technical specifications defining what was military and what could be allowed. All the German aircraft manufacturers immediately set about devising ways to circumvent the provisions of the Treaty and in this, Junkers was no less devious than the rest.

Indeed, one way of maintaining aircraft production seemed to be to transfer assembly abroad, so when an American, John Larsen declared that he wanted to build the F 13 under licence and market it in the United States, Junkers reacted with enthusiasm. However in November 1920, the Inter-Allied Control Commission impounded eleven F 13s which were crated and awaited shipment from Hamburg to the United States. They were not released until several months later after the Commission had been persuaded that the F 13 was really a civil airliner and not a military aircraft in disguise.

Meanwhile Junkers continued to pursue its goal of helping to set up foreign airlines by forming joint ventures in many European countries, as well as in Persia and the Soviet Union. Fortunately the F 13 continued to stay in the limelight by establishing more world records, while Junkers exploited the adaptability of the aircraft by fitting it for such roles as aerial photography, air ambulance and crop spraying, even modifying one to transport carrier pigeons.

The F 13 introduced a number of innovative safety features including seat belts and a 'frangible' undercarriage which would collapse in a crash-landing to avoid the aircraft turning over. Although there are several cases where passengers and crew walked away from a wreckage in which only the cabin remained in one piece, in 1930 an F 13 suffered an in-flight failure when a British-operated example broke up over Meopham, Kent. This led to the first application of a crash investigation method pioneered by the Royal Aircraft Establishment, Farnborough, where the wreckage was re-assembled and the accident ascribed to a failure in the tailplane.

The thick cantilever low wing of the F 13 was built up of nine duralumin tubular spars with transverse bracing to form a strong girder-like structure, covered with the corrugated stressed duralumin skin which long remained the unmistakable sign of a Junkers design.

Production-line techniques were adopted for the F 13 which was not only manufactured in quantity by Junkers in Germany, but also built under licence in Japan, Russia and the United States.

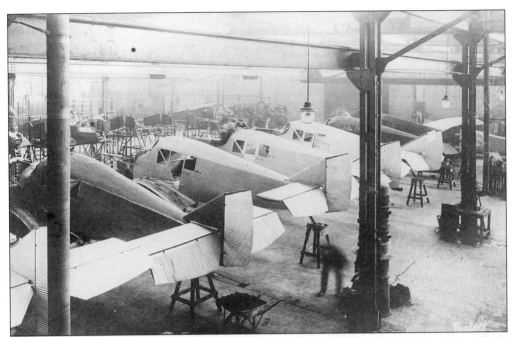

The F 13 revolutionised the construction of transport aircraft throughout the world and the basic design proved to be both highly adaptable and easily repaired.

At the peak of production one F 13 rolled off the line every week and some 322 had been built when it closed in 1932. However, just how many were built in Japan and the United States as well as by the Junkers branch works at Fili near Moscow, is uncertain. Some say that around 1,000 were produced in total, but this figure has never been confirmed.

Above: Although passengers in the F 13 were accommodated in a completely closed cabin, the two pilots flew the aircraft from a semi-enclosed cockpit which, initially, was without a windscreen. This arrangement was not uncommon in the early days of air transport but it obliged crews to wear flying suits. Later models of the F 13 were fitted with a windscreen and a baffle at the side to deflect the slipstream.

Left: With few exceptions, Junkers aircraft have been low-wing designs and the F 13, seen here with an A 20 – a later design largely used to carry mail – set the pattern for all airliners subsequently built by the company.

Junkers Ganzmetall-Flugzeug F13

The prototype F 13 was still flying with Lufthansa twenty years after its first flight on 25 June 1919, a remarkable demonstration both of the aircraft's durability and the fact that the designer got it right first time. Registered D-1 and named *Annelise*, the aircraft set a world record in September 1919 when it carried eight people to a height of 22,146 feet.

Sporting a modified tail, *Annelise* was included in a line-up of Lufthansa aircraft assembled at Berlin Tempelhof Airport in 1936 during the airline's tenth anniversary celebrations.

Carrying no more passengers than the average business jet of today, the F 13 was flown by Lufthansa on many domestic services in Germany and the airline continued to operate the type until 1940.

FLIEGT in die Bäder

During the summer season, Lufthansa operated the F 13 to spas and seaside resorts on the shores of the Baltic and North Seas, advertising services which became increasingly popular. This is an early example of scheduled air services operated mainly for tourists, although Junkers Luftverkehr (the company's own airline) was the first to begin F 13 floatplane services to Baltic seaside resorts in 1923.

It was not unusual for airlines to use beaches as landing strips during seasonal services to popular resorts, but wherever the F 13 was operated, ground crews were obliged to swing the propeller to start the engine. This was a hazardous task but one which could be accomplished without risk by skilled personnel.

During the turnround of an F 13, cleaners ensured that the cabin remained tidy and dust-free (evidently using a carpet beater if necessary), while an engineer checked the engine, topping up the oil and making adjustments as required.

When Lufthansa inaugurated a cargo service operated by the F 13 between Berlin and Istanbul on 1 May 1931, Bulgarian military aircraft flew a guard of honour as the aircraft flew over their territory.

Junkers formed an airline in Persia (Iran) which operated F 13s built in Fili near Moscow; some were fitted with a dorsal machine gun position to the rear of the cockpit, suggesting that air transport was not their sole function.

Formed in 1930 as a subsidiary company of Lufthansa in partnership with the Chinese government, Eurasia initiated services with F 13s. The airline continued to operate until the end of 1940.

24

Above: That the F 13 was highly adaptable is evident from this view of a ski-equipped version seen at Breslau Airport during a severe winter in 1928/29. Lufthansa was one of several operators which used the aircraft in this guise when snow conditions prevailed. It says much for the reliability of the engines of that time that the F 13 could operate scheduled services in freezing temperatures.

Right: Considerable agility was required of crews as they started the F 13 in winter conditions. Doubtless their leather flying suits were very necessary too!

Formed as a subsidiary of Lufthansa, with the support of the Chinese government, Eurasia brought air transport to some remote areas but because of the invariably rough condition of the airfields, special balloon tyres were fitted to the F 13. Needless to say, many hazards attended the pioneering flights made by Eurasia but the F 13, along with other Junkers types, proved to be durable in difficult conditions.

By contrast, the operations of Varig in Brazil posed quite a different challenge for the F 13 in terms of weather and terrain conditions. However, the F 13 was the first airliner to be exported to many countries around the world where it often pioneered new routes.

It was possible to make use of the Rhine and other waterways in the early days of air transport and on 16 May 1927, a Lufthansa F 13 floatplane inaugurated a service between Cologne and Rotterdam via Duisberg. The first flight is seen here being given a cheery wave from folk on the slipway.

Turkey was another country which operated the F 13 floatplane...

...while the Danube and Lake Balaton provided take-off and landing points for this Hungarian Aero Express floatplane.

Although the prototype F 13 somehow managed to carry as many as eight people on its record-breaking flight in 1919, for normal airline operations with only four on board it was thought prudent to weigh passengers and their baggage. This 1920 scene was routine at airports around the world in the early days of air transport.

Some agility was needed on the part of passengers when boarding the F 13, although steps built into the wing eased access. However, the cabin was comfortable with seating modelled on that of the motorcars of the day and from the earliest examples, passengers were provided with safety-straps – a feature which was not generally adopted until many years later.

A Lufthansa F 13 floatplane is seen here at Akureyri Bay on the north coast of Iceland to which it had flown on a charter during 1929. Such floatplanes were widely used in the pioneering days of air transport and during 1927, the Norddeutscher Lloyd ship *Lutzow* carried an F 13 floatplane to conduct pleasure flights during cruises.

Founded in Finland in 1923, with a financial contribution from Junkers Luftverkehr, Aero OY (which operates as Finnair today) was equipped with F 13 floatplanes.

Founded in 1919 with German capital and flown by German pilots, Sociedad Colombo Alemana de Transportes Aereos (SCADTA) was equipped with F 13 floatplanes.

Seen moored on the banks of the Rio Magdalena near Girardot, SCADTA F 13 floatplanes pioneered many services in South America.

In 1924 Deutsche Aero Lloyd and SCADTA established the Condor Syndicate which operated a number of floatplanes, including F 13s.

A few F 13s have survived to be preserved in museums in several countries and this example may be seen in the Stockholm Technical Museum, while others have been restored for display in Paris and Munich.

The remains of two F 13s which served with the Royal Flight of King Amanullah of Afghanistan in 1928 were discovered in a hangar at Kabul in 1969, and one has been completely rebuilt for the Deutsches Museum in Munich.

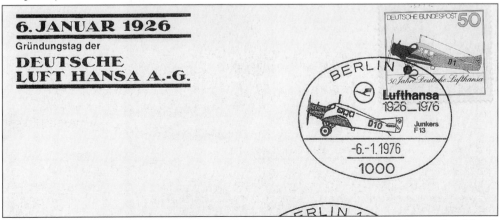

The F 13 was featured on a stamp issued in Germany in 1976 to celebrate the fiftieth anniversary of the foundation of Lufthansa.

One of two F 13s leased by Junkers to the Swiss operator Ad Astra Aero became the subject of a cause celebre when, on 20 October 1921, it was chartered by the former Austrian emperor, Karl IV for a flight to Geneva. However, piloted by a Junkers pilot Wilhelm Zimmermann, the aircraft flew the emperor and his wife out of exile to the Hungarian border town of Odenburg but in the event, the attempt to restore the Habsburg monarchy failed. Although Ad Astra was charged with conniving in the enterprise, the airline was able to absolve itself because Zimmermann was not its employee and had in effect 'hijacked' the aircraft and flown it to a different destination. The former emperor and his consort were arrested and banished to the island of Madeira, while Zimmermann was expelled from Switzerland back to Dassau. The F 13 was confiscated and today it can be seen in a Budapest museum.

The F 13 features in this poster designed by Alexander Rodchenko to promote the services of USSR-based Dobrolyet, one of the many airlines which Junkers helped to form in the 1920s and '30s. In 1988 the poster was Lot 8 in a sale organised by Sotheby's in Moscow, suggesting that such long forgotten items can eventually become quite valuable.

Three
Steps Towards a Giant Transport

Throughout the many years in which Hugo Junkers was involved in aviation, he was never happier than when engaged in research and the development of a new project. Indeed, as early as 1910 he took out a patent for a thick section wing envisaged as part of an aircraft which could cross the Atlantic in thirty-six hours; in 1914 he revealed his vision of giant aircraft with a capacity for a hundred, or even a thousand passengers.

Junkers was practical as well as visionary and by 1921 he had built a wing section for the JG 1 which was to have been the first of a series of very large aircraft. This component was never completed however, because of limitations imposed by the Versailles Treaty which forbade the construction of aircraft judged to have a military application, so construction of the four-engined, 36 metre wing span airliner which began in 1920 as Project 10, was abandoned a year later and the completed sections destroyed.

While the F 13 could be described as the culmination of a period in which research and development had proved the concept of all-metal construction and cantilever monoplane design, Junkers was conscious of the need to experiment further in order to gain the knowledge necessary to build a giant transport aircraft. To this end, he built up a team of experienced design engineers and pilots who worked together on turning new ideas into practical hardware.

But for the fact that it is known Junkers had specific projects in mind in 1920, it would be hard to believe that the aircraft which emerged from the Dessau workshops from then on were intended to be tangible steps towards the goal of building a giant transport aircraft. Not that the function of each model was to test some significant new development; after all Junkers needed to sell aircraft in order to fund his research. Nevertheless, many of the aircraft which were produced during the 1920s, did advance the company's knowledge and understanding of what after all, was still a very new technology. That an aircraft which was a giant of its time actually flew by 1929, is testimony to Junkers' determination to advance the 'state-of-the-art,' but historians also credit him with great foresight by also developing other innovative solutions, even though they were never built. For example Project 9, the 38-metre wing-span R 4 which preceded the JG 1 as a design study, was a three-engined aircraft in which the twenty-four passengers plus the crew were carried in the fuselage, while the control surfaces were mounted on twin booms which extended behind the wings.

Project 11, otherwise known as Junkerissime was intended to carry up to sixty-four passengers in each of two fuselages joined together by the 62.80 metre wing. Functioning as twin booms, the fuselages mounted the tail surfaces while the wing was thick enough to accommodate freight, mail and baggage, as well as the four engines which could be maintained during flight. The Junkerissime was proposed in both flying boat and landplane versions, with the former planned for trans-Atlantic services to be operated via the Azores, while in place of the hull shapes beneath the fuselage booms of the flying boat version, the landplane would have had three wheels. The J 1000, known as the 'giant duck', was the last of the studies and the 80 metre wing would have been thick enough to accommodate 100 passengers and a crew of ten. Control surfaces included rudders at the wing tips, while the elevator was mounted between the forward extremities of the twin fuselage in the 'canard' configuration increasingly preferred today – hence giant duck.

Some of these ideas were incorporated in the G 38 airline which flew for the first time in 1929, notably the facility for passengers to view the passing scene from observation rooms and indeed the 'engine room' of the aircraft was also located in the wing, enabling servicing to be carried out in flight by the engineers. Although only two G 38s were built, they attracted considerable attention when flown around Europe and were clearly regarded as symbols of German national prestige.

While Junkers clearly preferred low-wing designs, in the J 15, built in 1920, the company produced an experimental high-wing monoplane which was unusual in having no external bracing. The J 15 was also unusual in having an enclosed cabin for a single passenger with a cockpit for the pilot situated well aft in the fuselage.

The K 16, which appeared in 1921, was a logical progression from the J 15, being similar in layout although the pilot was positioned forward of the wing to enjoy a much better view, while the cabin was enlarged to carry two passengers. Eleven examples were built.

Said to have been developed as a two-seat research aircraft which could also be used for touring – an unlikely combination – the T 19 built in 1922, had a parasol wing set above the fuselage but was generally regarded to have had a poor performance.

It was comparatively rare for an aircraft manufacturer to produce aero engines as well, but Junkers drew on his earlier experience in the production of industrial gas-powered engines to design aircraft power plants. The early L1 seen here was produced in 1923 but did not fly until 1925, although by 1933 Junkers had produced its thousandth aero engine.

The T 21 was a further development of the T 19 and is believed to have been produced in quantity for the Red Army at the Junkers factory at Fili, near Moscow. The T 21 (sometimes referred to as the H 21) functioned primarily as a reconnaissance aircraft, but it could also carry bombs and machine guns. The single-seat H 22 fighter was similar to the T 21 but did not enter production.

Described as a multi-purpose aircraft, the A 20 was produced in 1923 as a mail-plane, for which Junkers reverted to the low-wing monoplane configuration. Produced in Germany and also at the Junkers' subsidiary in Sweden, the A 20 was both a landplane and sometimes fitted with floats. It is said to have served with operators in at least a dozen countries.

A total of forty-three A 20s were built and they could be fitted with wheels, floats or skis.

A further development of the T 19, the T 23 research aircraft, was unusual in appearing first as a bi-plane but was later converted to a parasol configuration. It was the first Junkers aircraft to be powered by a Le Rhone rotary engine.

The T 23 research aircraft first flew as a high wing monoplane but was later converted into a biplane by the installation of a small 'underwing'.

First flown in 1924, the G 23 tri-motor was subject to restrictions imposed by the Inter-Allied Control Commission which insisted that power should be limited to two 100 hp Mercedes D II engines on the wings, with a Junkers L2 of 195 hp in the nose. However thus powered, the performance of the first G 23 was barely adequate and subsequent models had engines of increased horsepower.

Produced in both landplane and floatplane versions, the G 23 served with several airlines including Ad Astra Aero of Switzerland. In order to avoid the restrictions imposed by the Allies, some G 23s were flown to Sweden where they were converted to G 24 configuration and given a Swedish registration before finding their way back to Germany!

No more than ten G 23s were produced and some were converted into the more powerful and slightly larger G 24, which achieved sales totalling fifty-six in all. First flown in 1925 powered by three Junkers L2a engines, the G 24 soon entered service with Lufthansa which, in addition to using them on scheduled European services, sent a pair to Peking and back in 1926.

Slightly larger than the G 23, the G 24 carried the same number of passengers and crew – nine and three respectively – but unlike the earlier tri-motor, the flight deck was fully enclosed. The G 24, seen here, towers over a tiny Messerschmidt Me 17 light aircraft.

The G 24 is said to have operated the first regular passenger flights by night, inaugurating a service between Berlin and Konigsberg on 1 May 1926. To ease the task of the pilots, tall buildings near Tempelhof were floodlit or marked by red lights, while every 25 to 30 kilometres rotating beacons marked the course to the northeast.

Less than six months after Lufthansa's foundation, two of its G 24s set off from Berlin bound for Peking – a 10,000 km journey which they covered in ten stages. Arriving on 30 August 1926, the first aircraft was quickly surrounded by Chinese spectators and resident Germans.

The crews of the G 24s were given a warm welcome on their arrival in Peking where they landed on a parade ground at Nanyun, but plans to continue to Shanghai had to be abandoned because of an armed rebellion.

Covering a total distance of some 20,000 km, the flights to and from Peking stimulated world-wide attention and the crews were feted on their return to Berlin on 26 September 1926. Unfortunately, later negotiations for a Trans-Eurasia route to Peking failed because of financial difficulties.

Although the early days of air transport may appear crude by today's standards, in 1928 passengers arriving in Berlin could immediately board a bus which took them to the city centre. This photograph shows passengers deplaning from a G 24 at Tempelhof.

Claimed to have been the first practical night mail service, in 1929 the German Post Office introduced regular flights from Berlin to London, Paris, Copenhagen, Malmo and Stockholm, employing G 24s operated by Lufthansa.

Already familiar with Junkers aircraft, during the 1930s the Syndicato Condor operated two G 24 floatplanes which flew mail between Recife and Rio de Janeiro, Brazil and on to Buenos Aires, Argentina.

First flown in 1933, the G 24 nao (also designated K 30) powered by three Siemens/Rhone Jupiter radial engines, was an experimental bomber which had a shorter wing span and other detailed modifications. Only one example was built at Dessau, but a further ten are said to have been built under licence in Malmo, Sweden.

First flown in 1928, the single-engined F 24 was the final derivative of the G 23 and it was powered by a number of different engines including a Junkers Jumo 204 diesel. A total of ten F 24s entered airline service – mostly with Lufthansa – and all were converted from G 23 or G 24 aircraft.

The two-seat T 29 was the first Junkers aircraft to feature the innovative full-span slotted flap and aileron assembly at the wing trailing edge - later to be included in the Ju 52 and many other designs.

A development of the G 24, the G 31 had a much larger fuselage which could accommodate fifteen passengers and the first of fifteen examples flew in 1928. The spacious cabin of the G 31 was also adapted to carry freight which could be loaded through a hatch in the roof and thus modified; two were operated in New Guinea to carry components for three complete dredgers for use in gold fields.

Lufthansa claims to have been the first airline to serve food and beverages to its passengers – made possible by the wide fuselage of the G 31 which became known as 'the flying dining car.'

The spacious cabin of the G 31 with its wide aisle, enabled the steward to attend to the needs of passengers without difficulty. On some aircraft, seats could be converted into sleeping berths.

Lufthansa established its own maintenance base at Berlin-Staaken Airport where G 31 engines are seen undergoing routine overhaul according to a fixed schedule, an early example of this now familiar system.

The Staaken facility also included an engine test stand controlled from within a cabin.

The K 39 is an example of the conversion of a civil design to a military role. Starting out in 1926 as the A 32 three-seat multi-purpose aircraft, it was flown to Sweden the following year to be given an armed reconnaissance role.

Functioning as a light bomber, the K 39 featured a ventral turret for the bomb aimer, while the rear-most of the three tandem open cockpits was fitted with a ring-mounted machine gun.

Developed in 1926 from the F 13, the W 33 proved to be a worthy successor, showing a similar adaptability to a wide variety of tasks; hence many were operated as floatplanes carrying passengers and cargo to remote areas. When production ended in 1934, a total of 199 had been built.

The W 33 secured a place for itself in aviation history when on 12 April 1928, a heavily laden, specially modified version took off from Baldonnel near Dublin, bound for America. Crewed by Herman Kohl, Ernst von Hunefeld and Major James Fitzmaurice (commander of the Irish Air Corps base, Baldonnel), the W 33 made the first non-stop east-west crossing of the Atlantic.

Understandably, the trans-Atlantic flight of the Bremen did much to raise the status of Junkers and the W 33, which attracted considerable attention at trade exhibitions.

With a 17.76 m wing span, the W 33 was a large single-engined aircraft and exhibition visitors (Berlin 1928?) were given an opportunity to see inside the cockpit.

Air cargo was intended to be the primary payload for the W 33 and it proved to be very efficient in this role, inaugurating Lufthansa's mail services for example. By contrast, the airline also used the W 33 to explore the possibility of opening services to the Far East.

Air freight was an important aspect of the early years of air transport and Lufthansa promoted its services by producing postcards and posters featuring the W 33.

A W 33 flew from Berlin to Irkutsk in Siberia and back in less than a week, crewed by flight engineer Fritz Eichentopf and pilots Joachim von Schroder and Erich Albrecht. The round trip confirmed the viability of such a service but unrest in Afghanistan resulted in King Amanullah being deposed before his plans to build airports could be put into effect, so an important link to the Far East could not be established.

Chinese soldiers were a common sight during Eurasia's W 33 reconnaissance flights as is evident from this scene at Urumchi near the Russian border, taken in the 1930s. These were turbulent times and warring factions added to the problems faced by the pilots and ground crews.

Maintenance facilities for Eurasia's W 33s were very basic but this bamboo-framed thatched 'hangar' enabled engineers to work on the engine under cover.

An Eurasia W 33 taking off from Lanchow airfield some 2,000 m above sea level. Special balloon tyres were fitted to F 13s and W 33s to ease operation from rough air strips, making them true 'bush' aircraft.

A W 33 is seen at Sonchow in the Gobi Desert, the aircraft performing well in such tough conditions, although on one expedition an aircraft was forced to land when Mongolian soldiers opened fire and injured one of the crew. Arrested and threatened with execution they were eventually released and returned to a hero's welcome.

Keen to operate by night as well as in poor weather conditions, in 1928 Lufthansa began to train its pilots for blind- and instrument-flying. For this, a W 33 was adapted as a trainer, with the student enclosed in the right section of the cockpit while the instructor in an open cockpit could maintain visual contact.

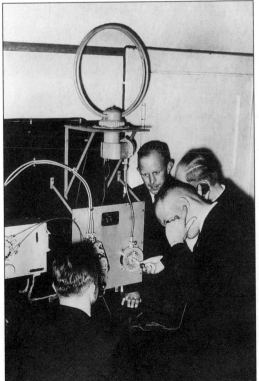

Instrument flying was taught in a classroom before pilots practised their skills in a real aeroplane. Training in wireless communication was also a classroom subject which helped to accelerate the introduction of scheduled flights by night.

Fitted with a more powerful engine than that installed on the W 33, the W 34 was similar in appearance except for the fact that it had windows for the passengers. This floatplane version operated by Canadian Airways was equipped to carry both passengers and cargo.

This W 34 floatplane which served in Canada for many years flew for the last time in September 1962 and is now preserved in the National Aviation Museum, Ottawa.

The W 34 was the type of rugged design which is ideal for Canadian conditions and this wheeled version seen at Sea Island, Vancouver International Airport, was operated by Pacific Western Airlines.

Powered by a BMW Hornet engine, this W 34 carries a civil registration but was probably used by the Luftwaffe as a navigation trainer, as well as for transport tasks. The last of the W 34s built was produced in Sweden in 1935.

For a time, the standard advanced flight trainer in service with the Luftwaffe, the W 34, was also used for blind flying instruction as well as to train radio operators. In addition to Luftwaffe markings, some aircraft carried a civil registration.

At the end of the Second World War, comparatively rare aircraft such as the W 34 (of which only 100 were built) were to be discovered in scrapyards on airfields around Germany. This example was photographed at Klagenfurt.

Developed as the successor to the A 20 mail aircraft, the A 35 was similar in configuration, although slightly shorter and fitted with a more powerful engine. First flown in 1926, about a couple of dozen were produced in both landplane and floatplane versions.

A military derivative of the A 35, the K 53 was built in Sweden to avoid the restrictions imposed by the Inter-Allied Aeronautical Commission, but only two were built. The Swedish-registered floatplane version seen here is thought to have served in Russia with the designation R 53.

A twin-engined light bomber which appeared in 1928 as the S 36 'mail carrier,' the K 37 was the subject of clandestine military trials because of restrictions then in force on the production of this type of aircraft. Development was carried out in Sweden and the first example was eventually transferred to the Luftwaffe, although series production was limited to Japan where 174 were built by Mitsubishi and Kawasaki.

As early as 1927, some W 34 freight aircraft were converted to K 43 standard at Limhamn near Malmo, Sweden. In this military guise, the K 43 served as a reconnaissance and patrol aircraft for which provision was made to carry depth charges or other weapons. Only small numbers were produced for the air forces of Finland and Columbia.

Only one A 48 was built in 1927 but it served as a prototype of the K 47 fighter, although, to complicate matters, trainer versions of the K 47 were also given the A 48 designation. Operated by a crew of two in tandem open cockpits, the A 48 was powered by a single 500 hp Jupiter engine produced by Siemens under licence from Bristol, although some later examples were fitted with the Pratt & Whitney Hornet, licence-produced by BMW.

The K 47 first flew in 1928 and was used to develop dive bombing techniques but never served in this role with the Luftwaffe. A dozen examples of the Hornet-powered version were purchased by the Chinese Air Force.

As early as 1914, Junkers considered the development of large airliners and in the 1920s, the company carried out studies for transport aircraft which were large even by today's standards. The twin fuselage flying boat seen here in model form was dubbed the Junkerissime and was intended to carry up to sixty-four passengers.

The Junkerissime featured the very thick wing which Junkers had in mind for most of his giant transport aircraft. One benefit of this arrangement was easy access to the engines so that they could receive attention during flight if necessary.

The Project 1,000 of 1924 was a curious design which was given the nickname 'Giant Duck' because its control surfaces were mounted between the forward part of the twin fuselages. The aircraft would have accommodated 100 passengers carried in the thick wing along with the crew and luggage.

When the G 38 flew for the first time in 1929, it was the culmination of Hugo Junkers' dream to produce a giant transport aircraft. Featuring the thick wing which was the subject of studies in the early 1920s, the G 38 carried only thirty-four passengers, although in addition to seats in the fuselage, observation rooms were also accommodated in the wing.

When the G 38 first appeared it was fitted with massive spats which all but covered the tandem main wheels, but these were later removed as they made no effective contribution to its performance. At first fitted with two different types of water cooled Junkers engines driving four-bladed propellers inboard and two-bladed propellers outboard, the G 38 was later standardised to four engines of equal power, each driving four-bladed propellers.

Only two G 38s were built and both eventually served with Lufthansa, although on delivery in June 1930, the first aircraft was not used in commercial service initially and was written off in a crash in 1936. However the second aircraft continued to operate scheduled flights until the outbreak of war in September 1939 but was destroyed in the ensuing conflict.

Despite being the largest landplane of its time, the G 38's bat-like wings enabled it to land at remarkably low airspeeds. Retractable oil and water radiators were another unusual feature of the Junkers giant which became a symbol of German prestige, undertaking extensive tours of Europe before entering regular operations with Lufthansa.

Judged by the Japanese Air Force to have the qualities of a heavy bomber, Junkers carried out the re-design work on the G 38 for this role under the designation K 51. The six examples which entered military service in the mid-1930s were built under licence in Japan by Mitsubishi as the Ki 20 and at least one was still operational in 1943.

The cockpit of the G 38 was equipped for operation by two pilots using large wheels which were mechanically linked to the flying controls. The seven-man crew comprised the captain, flight engineer/co-pilot, radio operator/navigator, chief engineer/engine mechanic, two assistant engineers and a steward.

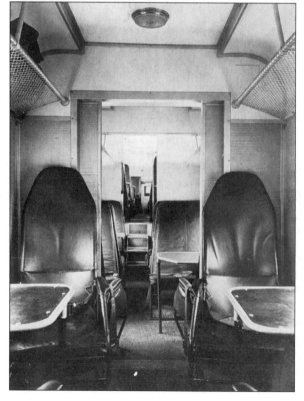

The cabin of the second G 38 was modified to include a second deck and seating was increased to accommodate thirty-four passengers. Two seats in the aircraft's nose afforded panoramic views, although passengers in the observation rooms in the forward part of the wing could also see ahead. Passenger facilities that were unusual for the time included a small smoking cabin, two washrooms and a galley.

Much of the space available in the G 38 was devoted to passenger comfort rather than the provision of more seats, so meal service was not the cramped affair customary on today's airliners. Indeed, once the aircraft was settled at its cruising altitude, passengers could leave their seats and walk around, visiting the observation rooms in the wing or the navigator's room, which also doubled as an observation platform.

In 1943, Lufthansa carried its millionth passenger and this was celebrated with due ceremony at Tempelhof from where, in times of peace, G 38s operated to Hanover and London, Copenhagen and Malmo, Halle/Leipzig, Nuremburg and Munich, Danzig and Konigsburg.

The giant G 38 dwarfed the next design from the Junkers drawing boards, the A 50 two-seat sports and touring aircraft which, like the airliner, flew for the first time in 1929 but went on to achieve fame for its long-distance flights.

This cutaway drawing of the G 38 reveals the interior layout of this remarkable aeroplane in which the thick wing was used to accommodate baggage, as well as fuel for the four engines which could be accessed during flight.

Sometimes known as the Junkers 'Junior', the A 50 had attractive lines and was produced with either a conventional undercarriage or as a seaplane, attracting orders from many parts of the world. This example was flown by a private owner in Finland for many years.

The same Finnish-registered A 50 aircraft has now been preserved and may be seen in a museum in Helsinki.

At one time, Junkers had visions of mass-producing the A 50 and marketing it to 'the upper middle class' through car dealers. However, a time of world economic recession was not propitious for such a venture and total sales were relatively modest. The example seen here was exported to Australia, while others were sold in Brazil, South Africa, Portugal, Switzerland, Japan and Finland.

1923

The humble beginnings of Berlin Tempelhof Airport are evident from this photograph taken in 1923 but it went on to become the base from which Junkers Luftverkehr operated before it became part of Lufthansa in 1926. Tempelhof continues to function as an airport today, although there are proposals to close it early in the twenty-first century.

By 1928, Tempelhof had become a thriving centre for Lufthansa operations but flying at that time was largely for a privileged few, as air fares were high by today's standards.

Four

'Aunt Ju'

In October 1930, the first flight of the Ju 52 took place – not the three-engined aircraft which was to secure a place for itself in aviation history years later, but a single-engined cargo transport. Indeed only five Ju 52s were built, one of these serving as a 15-seat passenger airliner, while the others were operated to carry cargo in both seaplane and wheel configurations, as far afield as Canada.

The realisation that the performance of the Ju 52 could be considerably enhanced by the use of more power led to the development of the Ju 52/3m (a designation indicating three engines) and the prototype of this version flew for the first time in May 1932. Indeed, from the outset Ernst Zindel had intended the development of a three-engined variant of the Ju 52 and undoubtably the lack of interest shown by Lufthansa in the single-engined model accounted for the accelerated introduction of the trimotor. In 1928, Zindel had been given the task of designing an entirely new transport aircraft which would have to be sufficiently inexpensive to buy, operate and maintain, without need of a subsidy.

Hugo Junkers had concluded that the greatest need for air transport was in remote parts of the world where surface links were poor, so the Ju 52 was also expected to be rugged and adaptable. While the first orders for the new trimotor came from operators in Columbia and Bolivia, it was not long before Lufthansa acquired its first example and ultimately around eighty Ju 52s were in operation with the airline by the end of the 1930s, the aircraft forming the backbone of its fleet. However, military interest soon led to its service with the Luftwaffe and the Ju 52 had its baptism of fire during the Spanish Civil War when it was used as a bomber.

But it was as a transport that the Ju 52 achieved its greatest fame and, including some constructed in France and Spain, a grand total of 4,835 were built, mostly for military service, although many 'demobilised' models saw service with airlines after the Second World War.

Canadian Pacific operated a single-engined Ju 52 both as a landplane with a wheeled undercarriage or skis, and as a seaplane on floats.

The single-engined Ju 52 had some of the characteristics of the bush aircraft which have been so important in opening up remote parts of Canada and this example was operated by Canadian Airways in 1931, before it was transferred to Canadian Pacific in 1942.

Although one of the first examples of the Ju 52 to be built, this Canadian-operated example proved to be highly durable, transporting passengers and cargo to remote regions of that vast country.

The more familiar trimotor Ju 52/3m became the backbone of the Lufthansa fleet during the 1930s and was operated regularly into Croydon which served as London's main airport at that time.

Lufthansa showed no interest in the original version of the Ju 52 but acquired around eighty of the trimotors for operation over its extensive route network.

Air traffic control was very basic even in the 1930s when by no means all aircraft were fitted with radios – not least because they were apt to be heavy and unreliable. So although the Ju 52

seen here carries radio aerials, it is being given take-off clearance by a much older means of communication – a flag.

This cutaway drawing of a Ju 52 shows it to be much closer to today's airliner configuration than the giant G 38 which preceded it. There is no room for smoking cabins or observation rooms but nevertheless, the 'Aunt Ju' was a practical design which proved to be highly adaptable.

The cabin of the Ju 52 provided comfortable accommodation for up to seventeen passengers or as many as eighteen fully equipped troops in rather more Spartan conditions. With a row of single seats each side of a central aisle, passengers had at least as much room as on contemporary airliners.

At the peak of production for Lufthansa, the apron at Tempelhof was dominated by the Ju 52 but the aircraft quickly found customers in other parts of the world as well.

Lufthansa's Ju 52s operated as far as the extreme ends of its network including Lima, Peru, where this example is pictured in 1938.

On 24 July 1937, Fritz W. Hammer formed the Sociedad Ecuadoriana de Transportes Aereos (SEDTA) which began operations with two Ju 34s chartered from Lufthansa, later acquiring Ju 52s.

Lufthansa eventually acquired a majority holding in SEDTA and the airline's Ju 52, with German crews, helped to open up South America for civil air transport. The aircraft attracted considerable interest wherever they landed.

A Ju 52 of SEDTA is seen at La Toma airport in the Ecuadorian mountains during celebrations for its opening. The three-engined aircraft boasted a performance which enabled it to fly over the snow-covered Andes without too much difficulty.

Syndicato Condor operated Ju 52 floatplanes during the 1930s carrying mail between Recife and Rio de Janeiro, Brazil and on to Buenos Aires, Argentina, the final link in a service which started from Berlin with a Zeppelin airship.

As well as being the founder of airlines in Columbia and Ecuador, Fritz Hammer was the driving force behind the establishment of facilities for mail-planes such as this Syndicato Condor Ju 52, seen out of its usual water-borne environment.

When major servicing was required for the Ju 52s of Syndicato Condor, they were put into a floating dry dock in Buenos Aires harbour.

Operated by Lufthansa-Peru, this Ju 52 seen taking off at Arequippa, linked the west coast of South America to the east coast and the airmail route to Europe.

As Lufthansa's 'workhorse' the Ju 52 established a record of safety and reliability on regular flights over the Alps but the Andes posed a greater challenge, and some aircraft were fitted with more powerful engines to enable them to fly above 23,000 ft. To assist the passage of its aircraft through the Cristo Redemptor pass, Syndicato Condor set up its own radio beacon.

The Ju 52 was widely used by airlines throughout South America including such countries as Argentina, Bolivia, Ecuador, Peru and Uruguay, but the largest number were to be found in Brazil, where Varig was among the operators.

On the other side of the world, Eurasia used a Ju 52 in June 1937 to extend the Peking – Canton mail route to Kai Tak Airport in Hong Kong where this photograph was taken. In the same year, Eurasia extended its Sian-Kuonming service to Hanoi in order to link up with the Indo-Chinese routes of Air France.

Formed in 1930 as a joint venture between Lufthansa and the Chinese government, the Eurasia Aviation Corporation was initially equipped with the F 13, the W 33 aircraft following a year later. However, in 1934 the first of three Ju 52s was delivered and by 1936, nearly seventy-five percent of services from Shanghai were operated by the trimotor aircraft.

With the exception of Shanghai with its paved aprons, most of the airports served by Eurasia were simply flat fields, which became a morass during the rainy season, as this Ju 52 found out when it became stuck in the mud at Chengdu airport. Alas, the water buffaloes failed to drag it out and eventually planks had to be laid beneath the wheels of the undercarriage.

Shanghai was well equipped with hangars and all the facilities necessary to carry out maintenance on the Eurasia fleet, including these Ju 52s.

On 24 August 1937, a Lufthansa Ju 52 set out from Kabul, Afghanistan, bound for Sian in China via a hazardous route through the Wakhan Pass between the Pamir mountains and the Hindu Kush. Two days later, another Ju 52 followed the same route and also succeeded in reaching Sian but the return journey was to be more hazardous.

The crew of the Ju 52 feared lost on the Pamir expedition – Baron von Gablenz, Robert Untucht and Karl Kirchhoff – received a hero's welcome on their return to Berlin.

The Pamir expedition over the roof of the world.

As if the challenge of climbing through the Wakhan Pass at nearly 18,000 ft was not enough, the fact that the flight passed over a war zone near the border with China did not become known until Von Gablenz was obliged to make a forced landing on the return journey. He had taken off from Sian bound for Kabul and on to Berlin, but the port engine soon began to gulp oil and it was clear that the Ju 52 would not make it over the Pamirs.

An emergency landing was made on a field at Lob Bazar, near the caravan town of Chotan which was under the control of the thirty-sixth Tunganese Division. Having changed the spark-plugs on the ailing engine, Von Gablenz taxied out to take-off but abandoned the flight when bullets smashed into the cockpit and mounted soldiers made it clear that the aircraft should stop. Indeed, they continued firing, even after the crew scrambled from the Ju 52 with their hands raised in surrender.

Fortunately the soldiers' aim was poor, but the captured crew was carted off to the citadel in Chotan to suffer interrogation, hardship and privation at the hands of a general who showed no signs of granting them their liberty. Fortunately, a friendlier general gained the upper hand in clashes with their captors and a month after being taken prisoner the crew were given permission to continue their journey.

Despite the weak and spluttering port engine, the aircraft made the return to Kabul where the lost flyers were given a warm welcome, although an even warmer reception awaited them at Berlin to which they returned in a replacement Ju 52.

The hazards of flying over hostile territory led to a Eurasia Ju 52 being attacked by fighters during a flight from Hanoi to Kuonming, forcing it to crash-land on the side of a mountain. The starboard wing and undercarriage were torn away and the crew had to carry their wounded captain through the jungle for five days before they reached help.

Unwilling to abandon the damaged Ju 52, an expedition was mounted by a party of mechanics and thirty-three pack-horses carrying spare parts, as well as enough food for the hundreds of coolies needed to level enough soil to make a runway. Needless to say, it was a massive undertaking but after several months the aircraft and runway were ready.

Six months after the crash landing, the repaired Ju 52 – seen here helping to level the runway – lumbered slowly into the air and made for the nearest airfield which it reached without further difficulty.

Although occasionally used as a bomber and even to detonate magnetic mines, it was mainly as a transport aircraft that the Ju 52 was used by the Luftwaffe during the Second World War. Indeed, by far the greater number of Ju 52s built were for military service.

At the end of the war, the many Ju 52s which survived were pressed into service with those victorious forces which wanted them. Others joined the air forces of liberated countries to form the basis of new transport squadrons, some remaining in service for at least ten years. In all, of 180 Ju 52s which survived in airworthy condition, 137 were made serviceable to fly again.

The French Air Force operated many Ju 52s after the war, although most of these had been built in France by Ateliers Aeronautiques de Colombes which produced more than 400. This example was photographed at RAF Idris, Libya, in August 1958.

The Ju 52 first saw military service during the Spanish Civil War in 1936 but the aircraft was subsequently manufactured there by CASA which produced a total of 170, one of which is seen here in service with the Spanish Air Force.

Already in widespread use with European airlines before the Second World War, the Ju 52 resumed a civilian role after the conflict, although the Swiss Air Force operated three throughout the war, and these retired for civil use after forty-three years of service.

Although primarily used to train observers and radio operators, Swiss Air Force Ju 52s also carried out many transport duties, including the provision of aid to folk in mountainous regions cut off by avalanches.

As late as 1955, new roles were being found for the Ju 52 and this example was photographed at Dusseldorf Airport in 1955 before delivery to Sepik Airways for service in Papua New Guinea.

Several Ju 52s were acquired by Britain after the war and although most served with military operators, for a while British European Airways operated ten on domestic routes during 1946/7.

During the war a number of Ju 52s were shot down by Swedish anti-aircraft guns but some landed safely to be placed on the civil register. However, A.B. Transport acquired seven directly from Junkers including this floatplane.

In 1974 a small group of airmen at RAF Gatow, Berlin, undertook the restoration of a Ju 52/3m.

Originally built in Spain in 1944, the Ju 52 was brought back to pristine condition by the Royal Air Force team in Germany for non-flying display in Lufthansa colours.

Iron Annie was discovered in 1962 in poor shape in a corner of Quito airport where it had been abandoned after five years of service over South American jungles. Restored to flying condition by Martin Caidin, an American old-aircraft enthusiast, the Ju 52 appeared at air displays but was sold to Lufthansa in 1984 and flown to the airline's maintenance base at Hamburg.

The aircraft was stripped down, completely re-built, fitted with fourteen passenger seats and transformed into a certificated airliner once again so that Lufthansa could use it to carry fare paying aviation enthusiasts or guests on promotional tours. It has been painted in the airline's 1930s livery, but is equipped with modern avionics to conform to present-day requirements.

Hugo Junkers' enthusiasm for research and development attracted increasing criticism from within his company because it was seen to be draining money from aircraft production – which was not making money in the late 1920s anyway. However, in 1928 the German aviation research institute issued a requirement for a high altitude research aircraft, for which Junkers was awarded a contract. Believing that research should be self-financed from profits, Junkers had previously begun the development of a high-altitude version of the L-88 engine, although this was not ready in time for the first flight of the Ju 49 research aircraft. This flew for the first time on 2 October 1932, three years after development began, and it incorporated a pressurised cabin for the crew of two. With only a couple of portholes in the cabin, the pilot's view was somewhat limited, so a periscope was fitted to the floor to permit a view of the ground. Fitted with the definitive 800 hp engine, the Ju 49 gradually reached greater heights and in 1935 achieved 42,653 feet. It is generally accepted that the experience gained from this research programme proved useful a year later when the EF 61 high altitude research aircraft began flight trials, while the reconnaissance version of the Ju 86 bomber included a pressurised cockpit for the crew.

Five

War Again –
and the Final Chapter

The Junkers company, in common with other German aircraft manufacturers, did much to elude the activities of the Inter-Allied Aeronautical Commission of Control, established to enforce restrictions on aircraft production imposed under the Versailles Treaty. However, Junkers was more concerned with the inhibitions on the technical development of aviation than a desire to produce military aircraft. Nevertheless, bearing in mind that a number of military aircraft of Junkers design were produced in Sweden or Russia during the disarmament period which followed the First World War, some might take the view that the company was by no means disinterested in warplanes. The giant transport studies initiated by Junkers during the 1920s, together with the undoubted success of both the F 13 and Ju 52 as leading airliners of their day, support the claim that the company's interest lay primarily in the civil sphere.

By the early 1930s, the world economic recession had hit Germany particularly hard and Hugo Junkers was faced with an increasingly serious financial situation. Yet he refused to countenance the sale of his patents in order to pay off debts and this drew widespread criticism – even from within the company. Two days after the Nazi party assumed power in 1933, Junkers was 'requested' to hand over patent rights to the aviation ministry but the Professor refused. Following the arrest of three senior members of the Junkers staff who were expelled from Dessau and the initiation of 'investigations' into the Professor's eldest son and daughter, he gave in to this psychological pressure and surrendered the patents. That was by no means the end of the matter however, because the government expected German aircraft manufacturers to support the Third Reich and to devote their energies to the production of military designs.

Declaring that he was primarily interested in scientific research and that he alone would decide what his company would do, Junkers was once again at loggerheads with the new regime. Indeed, it was not long before he was accused of 'treason' by the Dessau public prosecutor and Junkers was summoned from his country home to attend 'consultations.' Faced with the alternative of agreeing to the disposal of his holdings in the aircraft and engine companies or being prosecuted, the 74 year old Junkers once again succumbed to blackmail. Even so, he was placed under virtual house-arrest and the prosecutor set about producing a report listing 'evidence' of his failings in order to counter efforts to rehabilitate the Professor. The 'Junkers case' dragged on, but on 3 February 1935 the old man died, although by then the appearance of the swastika on his former company's aircraft made no secret of where the direction of its efforts lay.

Little attempt was made to pretend that faster 'airliners' then coming off the drawing boards were not merely the forerunners of bombers and, from the mid-1930s until the end of the Second World War, the design and production skills of the Junkers aircraft and motor works were to be devoted to the war effort. Indeed, the Ju 87 dive bomber with its distinctive cranked wing, played an important part in the invasion of Poland and later proved to be a highly effective component in bringing about the collapse of French resistance in 1940.

Like the Ju 87, work on the Ju 88 bomber began several years before the outbreak of war but both remained in production throughout the conflict and, in addition to developing new combat aircraft, the company continued to produce the ubiquitous Ju 52 which served in large numbers mainly on transport duties. The Ju 287 four-engined jet bomber proved to be not only the last Junkers design to fly but also the final aircraft to bear its name. Occupied by Russian forces, the Dessau plants disappeared along with the Junkers name, closing the final chapter in the story of a once-famous company.

Derived from the W 34, the Ju 46 floatplane was operated by Lufthansa to carry mail to the United States after being catapulted from the deck of the Norddeutscher liners *Europa* and *Bremen*, some 1,200 km from the American coast.

Introduced into service in the mailplane role in 1932, the floatplane version of the Ju 46 could deliver the mail some twenty-four hours before the liner docked. Bearing the name of the vessels from which they were catapulted, the aircraft were painted red so that they could be more easily spotted if they had to make an emergency landing on water.

Operated by compressed air, the 27 metre long K2 catapult mounted amidships between the two funnels, launched the Ju 46 into the air far enough for it to pick up speed under its own power, provided by a 600 hp BMW radial engine.

In 1932, a Ju 46 floatplane flew services to seaside resorts on the North and Baltic Seas, proving to be highly popular. Only four Ju 46s were built and some ended their days as land-planes, including one operated in Brazil by Syndicato Condor.

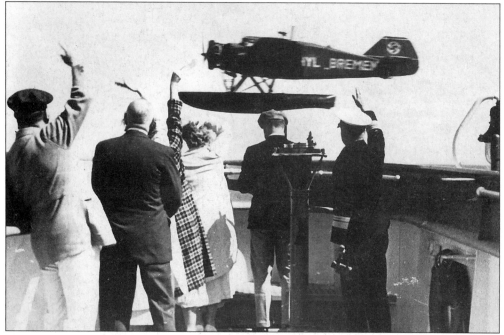

Safely launched, a Ju 46 is seen flying past the luxury liner Bremen before setting course for the North American coast. This method of speeding mail across both the North and South Atlantic was perfected during the 1930s.

Seen here dwarfed by the liner *Europa*, its Ju 46 mailplane operated an average of seventeen flights per year from the vessel in the period 1932 to 1935.

The last aircraft to be developed and produced by the company in 1931 whilst still under the direction of Hugo Junkers, the Ju 60 high-speed airliner, proved to be another example of his all too familiar obsession with advancing technology without actually making money. Of the four built, it is believed that only three entered service with Lufthansa.

Featuring the oval-section structure first employed on the A 50, the Ju 60 marked a departure from the Junkers tradition of using a corrugated skin overall, the fuselage and part of the tailplane being covered with a smooth alloy.

Seen here with an F 24 in the background, the Ju 160 was essentially the production version of the Ju 60 with corrugated skinning entirely replaced by smooth duralumin sheeting. A total of forty-eight Ju 160s were produced, the type entering service with Lufthansa in 1935 as a fast airliner with accommodation for six passengers.

Here being refuelled, this Ju 160 was one of a fleet of twenty-one operated by Lufthansa to provide express services on thirteen domestic routes. Powered by a 660 hp BMW radial engine, the Ju 160 could achieve a maximum speed of 211 mph, doubtless helped by the fully retractable undercarriage.

An early example of a Ju 86 airliner, powered by Junkers Jumo 205 diesel engines, is seen on the apron at Tempelhof. On the original copy of this photograph the swastika on the tail of the aircraft could have been seen.

Shown in silhouette, the full span slotted aileron and flap assembly can be clearly seen in this view of the Ju 86 which flew for the first time in 1934.

The 600 hp Junkers Jumo 205 diesel engine powered the first Ju 86 which, in its airliner form, could carry ten passengers and about fifteen served with Lufthansa. While South African Airways took delivery of eighteen Ju 86s starting in 1937, all were later transferred to the South African Air Force.

Although Lufthansa's Ju 86s operated mainly on many domestic services and over shorter European routes, in 1936 one specially modified model flew non-stop between Dessau and Bathurst in the Gambia, a distance of 5,797 km.

Two Lufthansa Ju 86s are seen here at the airline's Hamburg maintenance base.

Switzerland was one of the early customers for the Ju 86 airliner and Swiss Air Lines operated two on night mail services in the late 1930s.

The benefits of German airline activity in the Far East typified by the Eurasia venture, may be judged by the fact that Manchurian Airlines was a customer for some of the sixty civil variants of the Ju 86 before production switched to bomber and reconnaissance aircraft. Previously transported to Fongtien East airfield for assembly and flight tests, one of the Manchurian Ju 86s is seen here at Hsinching Airport.

A total of some 810 military Ju 86s were produced and the Royal Swedish Air Force purchased no less than forty from Junkers, with a further sixteen being built in Sweden by Saab. However, in Luftwaffe service the Ju 86 was not a notable success as a bomber, although as a high altitude reconnaissance aircraft capable of operating up to 41,000 ft, it fared rather better.

Some of the Swedish Ju 86s were converted to a transport role and one such example is seen here at Hatfield in the late 1940s, where it had brought pilots to collect some Vampire fighters.

First flown in 1937, the design of the Ju EF 61 high-altitude research aircraft differed significantly from that of the Ju 49 which preceded it by six years. Specifically, unlike the all-metal Ju 49 with its fixed gear and single engine, the EF 61 was powered by two engines, had a retractable undercarriage and was fabric covered except for the pressurised forward fuselage. Although two EF 61s were built and flown, they did not complete their flight trials because both aircraft crashed before a full performance assessment could be completed. Nevertheless, it was seen to be a step towards the development of high-altitude variants of the Ju 86 introduced in 1941.

The Sturzkampsflugzeug, better known as the Stuka became a key element in the *blitzkreig* invasions in the early years of the Second World War, a screaming siren attached to the starboard undercarriage leg, adding to the terror of those being dive-bombed. A total of no less than 5,709 Ju 87s were built but its effectiveness waned because it was relatively slow and ill-equipped to defend itself against more agile fighters. (Credit IWM)

Prototype Ju 87s bore a civil registration but there could be no doubting the purpose of an aircraft dedicated to dive-bombing. Initially produced to enter a competition against designs submitted by Arado, Blohm & Voss and Heinkel, the Ju 87 won the day because its ruggedness was considered to be superior.

While prototype Ju 87s were powered by Rolls-Royce Kestrel engines, all production models were fitted with Junkers Jumo engines of various power. Three early production models participated in the Spanish Civil War but with the exception of some supplied to the Italian Air Force, all were operated by the Luftwaffe.

A formation of Ju 87s was certain to strike terror into ground forces and dive bombing proved to be more accurate than horizontal attacks, although to prevent loss of control if the pilot 'blacked out' because of high 'g' forces, an auto-pilot took over during the pull-out phase.

Above: This Ju 87 was fitted with an unusual overwing passenger cabin which could hardly have enhanced an already somewhat sluggish performance.

Left: The 640 hp Junkers Jumo 210C powered early production models of the Ju 87, while other developments of this engine, the most powerful of which produced 1,300 hp, were selected for the three further models which followed.

After the war some captured Ju 87s were restored and this example was photographed at RAF Henlow in 1968.

Also to be seen at Henlow in 1968 was this 'Stukafied' Percival Proctor which proved to be a remarkably convincing Ju 87 replica!

Work on the development of a high-speed medium bomber began in 1935 under the designation Ju 85, but development beyond the mock-up stage led to the Ju 88 which differed principally in having a single fin and rudder instead of the twin arrangement on the first design. The prototype Ju 88 flew for the first time in 1936 and like the other test aircraft which followed, it carried a civil registration.

The Ju 88A bomber was the first production model but a total of 14,980 had been manufactured by the end of the war and variants included day and night fighters, as well as reconnaissance aircraft.

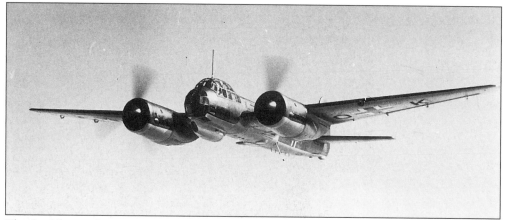

The Ju 88 was the nearest German equivalent to the de Havilland Mosquito in terms of versatility and it was equally effective as a bomber, fighter or reconnaissance aircraft.

Seen in Finnish Air Force markings, this Ju 88 was probably supplied to boost Finland's forces during the war with Russia.

This Ju 88A4 bomber powered by Junkers Jumo 211J engines was forced down in Switzerland in 1943 and 'interned.' It was one of many Luftwaffe (and Allied) aircraft which strayed into Swiss air space and were subsequently captured.

Right: Damaged aircraft which managed to crash-land without breaking up, such as this Ju 88, provided the Allies with an opportunity to compare German technology with their own.

Above: The wreckage of a crash-landed Ju 88 inevitably attracted attention and it was usually necessary to erect a cordon to allow a careful inspection, not least to ensure that the aircraft was safe to be moved.

Left: Captured virtually undamaged, this Ju 88 is seen being dismantled by RAF engineers to determine what lessons could be learned about the enemy's equipment.

After the end of the Second World War, there was considerable interest in the equipment which had been used in the conflict and Horse Guards Parade in the heart of London was the site of one exhibition of captured aircraft, including this Ju 88.

Fighter variants of the Ju 88 were fitted with a metal nose cone in place of the glazed structure featured on the bombers. This housed a cannon in addition to machine guns, while the turret under the nose housed a rearward-firing gun.

To achieve an improved high altitude performance, the Ju 188 incorporated an extended wing and other detailed modifications. Over 1,000 Ju 188s were built and it proved to be a versatile aircraft which was produced in fighter, bomber, reconnaissance and torpedo-bomber variants.

Slender wings with pointed tips were a feature of the Ju 188, a characteristic of high-altitude aircraft at that time.

Although clearly derived from the Ju 88, the high altitude Ju 188 had a completely re-designed cockpit canopy of more aerodynamic shape. To reduce their vulnerability to enemy night fighters, engine flame dampers were installed on some variants.

Among the captured aircraft acquired by the USAF Museum, the Ju 188 is an example of a widely-used Junkers design which was developed for such high-altitude roles as photo-reconnaissance, fighter and bomber. Over 1,000 Ju 188s were built between September 1941 and the end of the war.

Only twenty-two Ju 288 medium bombers were built, although most of these were prototype or development aircraft, distinguished by their elongated glazed nose and twin fin and rudder configuration. Work on this Ju 88 derivative began in 1940 but in response to a greater need for fighter aircraft, development of the Ju 288 bomber ended in 1943.

The Ju 388 reverted to the single fin and rudder of the Ju 88 and Ju 188 and although originally intended to be a fighter development of the latter, reconnaissance and bomber variants were also built and tested. However, only the reconnaissance version, fitted with three cameras and armed only by a single rearward-firing machine gun, entered squadron service.

The last derivative of the Ju 88, the Ju 388 was initially intended to be a fighter, although the first prototype was built in 1943 as a reconnaissance aircraft. Indeed, the third prototype was built as a bomber and a torpedo-bomber version was proposed but never completed. Only reconnaissance Ju 388s were built but a few saw service in the closing months of the war before this example was flown to RAE Farnborough, along with several other captured German aircraft.

The USAF Museum is the final home of this Ju 388: one survivor of the little more than thirty that were built. Combining aspects of the Ju 188 and Ju 288, the aircraft featured the single fin and rudder of the former and the glazed elongated nose of the latter.

The prototype Ju 90, which flew for the first time in 1937, was unusual in having been developed from the Ju 89 bomber which was produced a year earlier (a reversal of the usual process). The Ju 89 was destroyed in an accident and the Luftwaffe thereafter showed a preference for smaller, faster bombers. As a 40-seat airliner however, the Ju 90 was an advanced design with such features as a retractable undercarriage and a spacious cabin.

The prototype Ju 90 was powered by four DC 600 inverted-vee, liquid-cooled engines but production models were fitted with BMW radial engines.

The Ju 90 was to be the last civil airliner produced by Junkers. Lufthansa operated a fleet of

eleven at one time, although most were pressed into military service on the outbreak of war.

The prototype Ju 90, with its liquid-cooled engines, featured radiator doors which could be opened or closed as required. The radiators in this view are shown with the doors closed, providing less drag when not needed.

With the radiator doors opened, the cooling system for the engines was activated, although this function added to the tasks on the flight deck.

The distinctive Junkers slotted flap and aileron can be clearly seen in this view of the Ju 90, the swept-backed leading edge of the wing also being evident. This aircraft was the first to enter service with Lufthansa and may be one of two which were returned to the airline in 1940, after all had been initially taken into service with the Luftwaffe.

After a short period of service with Lufthansa, this Ju 90 was made over to the Luftwaffe for use as a general transport aircraft, while others were used as development aircraft for the larger Ju 290.

In another example of Junkers' innovation, the engines of the Ju 90 were mounted in such a way that they could be changed in just half an hour, as demonstrated here for the benefit of the press. The engine and propeller were removed as a single power pack, speeding the process of replacement.

The 830 hp BMW 123H engine powered production models of the Ju 90 which could cruise at 200 mph.

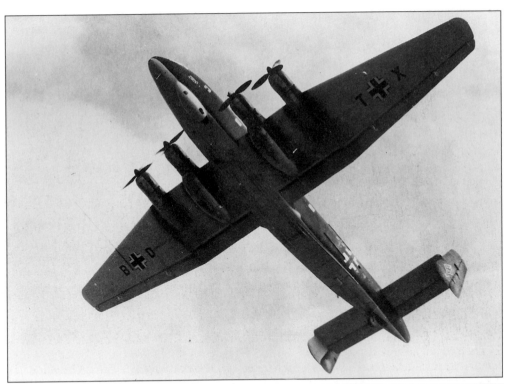

The Ju 280 was a logical progression from the Ju 89/90 and development began in 1940. Designed for heavy transport and maritime reconnaissance roles, some fifty-five Ju 290s were produced, including a significant percentage in Letov, Czechoslovakia.

For its day, the cockpit of the Ju 290 was well set-out and uncluttered. Capable of carrying up to forty-eight paratroops in its transport role, the Ju 290 was later developed into a bomber fitted with a gun turret in an elongated nose. However, only eighteen bombers were built and one was flown to the United States after the end of the war.

The giant Ju 390 powered by six 2,000 hp engines had a range of nearly 5,000 miles.

Only two examples of the Ju 390 long-range transport aircraft were built - at the Letov plant in Czechoslovakia - but a proposed reconnaissance version armed with fourteen machine guns never materialised.

As a tri-motor design, the Ju 252 was clearly derived from the Ju 52 but there the resemblance ends, as the all-metal construction did not feature the corrugated skin of the latter.

The Ju 252 could accommodate up to thirty-two troops and its performance was boosted by the retractable undercarriage which reduced drag. Although only fifteen were built, the Ju 252 was among the fleet of transport aircraft used to supply German forces in North Africa in 1942.

Similar in many respects to the earlier large trimotor, the Ju 352 featured fabric-covered wooden wings, these materials being used in order to save metal which was in short supply. Some of the forty-four Ju 352s built survived the war to fall into the hands of the Allies who learned that it was the first German aircraft to use reverse pitch propellers.

Junkers' earlier design work on giant airliners found an application in the Ju 322 military cargo glider project which was initiated early in the war. Like the G 38, the glider had a large, not to say massive, centre section of what was almost a flying wing. Certainly the wing was designed to accommodate bulky cargo which could be loaded directly into the hold through a huge doorway in the leading edge. The function of the short fuselage was simply to mount the tail surfaces but although two examples were built, and work on production models had begun, the programme came to an abrupt end when the first prototype crashed on its maiden flight, towed behind a Ju 90.

The Ju 287 was the last new Junkers aircraft to fly and like many which the company had produced before, it was of unorthodox design. Featuring forward-swept wings and a novel way of mounting the four engines – two on each wing and two on the forward fuselage – the first of two Ju 287s built flew for the first time in February 1945. However, the war ended before the trials were completed and production could begin.

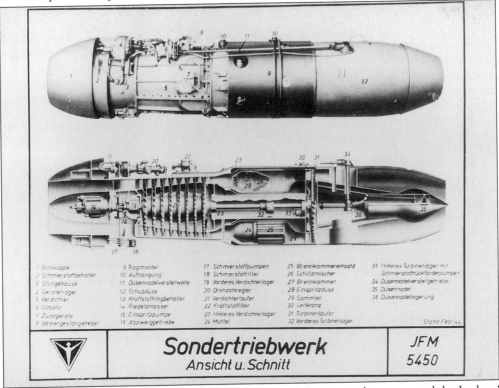

1 Stirnkappe	9 Tragmantel	17 Schmierstoffpumpen	25 Brennkammereinsatz	33 Hinteres Turbinenlager mit
2 Schmierstoffbehälter	10 Aufhängung	18 Schmierstoffilter	26 Schlitzmischer	Schmierstoffrückförderpumpen
3 Stirngehäuse	11 Düsennadelverstellwelle	19 Vorderes Verdichterlager	27 Brennkammer	34 Düsennadelverstellgetriebe
4 Geräteträger	12 Schubdüse	20 Drehzahlregler	28 Einspritzdüse	35 Düsennadel
5 Verdichter	13 Kraftstoffringbehälter	21 Verdichterläufer	29 Sammler	36 Düsennadellagerung
6 Ölmotor	14 Riedelanlasser	22 Kraftstoffilter	30 Leitkranz	
7 Zündgeräte	15 Einspritzpumpe	23 Hinteres Verdichterlager	31 Turbinenläufer	
8 Bediengestängehebel	16 Abzweiggetriebe	24 Muffel	32 Vorderes Turbinenlager	Stand Febr.44

Sondertriebwerk
Ansicht u. Schnitt

JFM
5450

Four Junkers Jumo 004 turbojets powered the Ju 287 and they not only represented the Junkers' contribution to the beginning of the jet age in aviation but also the end of the company, which soon faded into oblivion. Almost all Junkers plants were located in the part of Germany occupied by Soviet forces and although some personnel worked in Russia, the disappearance of the company was one of the many casualties of war.

Professor Dr Hugo Junkers, born 3 February 1859 – died 3 February 1935.

Acknowledgements

But for a suggestion made by Derek James, I should not have considered compiling a pictorial history of Junkers, although having been on the staff of Lufthansa for twenty years, I was aware of the importance of aircraft such as the F 13 and Ju 52. More importantly, I was also aware that Lufthansa maintained an excellent photograph archive from which I could probably secure many illustrations.

And so it proved. Consequently, thanks are due to Lufthansa for the many of the photographs of transport aircraft in this book, although even after contributions from SAS, Swissair and Canadian Airlines International, many gaps would have remained. However, Hans-Ulrich Willbold delved deeply into the Daimler-Benz Aerospace archives to provide a substantial number of rare photographs for which I am very grateful.

A publication of this kind can gain considerably from the contributions of aviation enthusiasts and in Mike Hooks I could not have wished for more support in this regard. Indeed, not only did he supply me with many photographs from his enormous collection, but he also provided much of the source material from which I have endeavoured to pour the proverbial quart into a pint pot. Thanks are also due to the Trustees of the Imperial War Museum for their permission to reproduce a particularly dramatic photograph.

Any publication of this kind must rely on team work and I am grateful for the patience and forbearance shown by David Buxton and his colleagues at Chalford Publishing, while to my wife Audrey, particular thanks are due for tolerating a mass of papers and photographs about the house, as well as casting a critical eye over the text.